DISNEY PRINCESS

Tiana's Cookbook

RECIPES
Joy Howard, Deanna F. Cook, and Cynthia Littlefield,
with additional recipes by Amy Croushorn, Cristina Garces, and Ariane Resnick

PHOTOGRAPHY
Joe St. Pierre and Joanne Schmaltz, with additional photography by Ken Carlson, Joanna Chattman,
Teri Lyn Fisher, Jacqueline Hopkins, Sandy Rivlin, Amy Croushorn, Becky Sharp, and Jean Allsopp

FOOD STYLING
Ann Lewis and Edwina Stevenson, with additional styling by Amy Croushorn,
Jenny Park, and Jennifer Pet

ILLUSTRATIONS
Elizabeth Tate and the Disney Storybook Art Team

DESIGN
Megan Youngquist

Special thanks to Simon Pearce for use of pottery, glassware, and other accessories on pages
4, 7, 28, 33–34, 56, 68, 81–82, 96, 98, 106, 108, 116, and 123

Printed in the United States of America
First Hardcover Edition, October 2009
Second Hardcover Edition, September 2022
1 3 5 7 9 10 8 6 4 2
Library of Congress Control Number: 2009926905
FAC-034274-22203
ISBN 978-1-368-07496-4
Visit www.disneybooks.com

DISNEY PRINCESS

Tiana's Cookbook

DISNEY PRESS

Los Angeles • New York

Contents

Get Ready to Cook—Just like Tiana!

Tiana has always loved cooking. When she was a little girl, she and her daddy, James, would stir up a pot of gumbo together, using whatever was in the cupboard. Their food always brought people together—the family's neighbors would visit as soon as they caught a whiff! And when Tiana grew up, these wonderful memories inspired her to pursue her dream: opening her own restaurant.

After years of hard work, Tiana made her dream come true when she opened the jazz-filled restaurant Tiana's Palace in New Orleans! A couple pieces of advice helped her along the way:

- You're never too young to start learning your way around the kitchen.
- Real ingredients are important, but one secret ingredient makes every dish taste even better: love.

Now it's your turn to get cooking! Turn the page to discover recipes that would fit right in on the menu of Tiana's Palace—from breakfast, lunch, and dinner, to beverages, snacks, and desserts. The recipes are rated on a five ❋ scale, so if you're a beginner, don't worry! Start with an easier dish {❋} and work your way up to the more complicated recipes {❋ ❋ ❋ ❋ ❋}.

Before You Begin

Cooking is a lot of fun, but before you get started, there are some important things to remember. Always, always ask a parent for permission. Even Tiana was a beginner once—and she always asked her daddy for help before she used the kitchen. If you need to use a stove, oven, blender, or mixer for a recipe, make sure to ask an adult to help you. Here are a few other tips to keep in mind.

- If you have long hair, tie it back. You don't want it to end up in the food or near a hot stove.

- Make sure your clothing isn't loose enough to touch a stovetop burner. If you're wearing long sleeves, push them up to your elbows.

- Put on an apron to keep your outfit from getting stained.

- Wash your hands with water and soap for at least twenty seconds so they will be clean when you handle the ingredients.

- Take a few minutes to read the whole recipe so that nothing will come as a surprise once you get started.

- Gather all the equipment you'll need, such as measuring spoons, bowls, baking pans, and utensils, before you get out the ingredients.

Measuring Ingredients

To make sure a recipe turns out just the way it's supposed to, you need to measure ingredients exactly. Here are some helpful hints and tips.

- For liquids like milk, water, or oil, use a measuring cup with a spout designed for pouring.

- A dry ingredient, such as flour, sugar, or cocoa, should be spooned into a measuring cup without a spout. Then, to check that you have the exact amount, scrape the flat edge of a butter knife across the rim of the cup to remove any extra.

- A chunky ingredient should be spooned into a measuring cup and then patted gently, just enough to even out the top without packing it down. Shredded ingredients are also measured this way.

- Brown sugar should be packed into measuring cups to press out any air bubbles.

- Measuring butter is really easy if you use sticks that have tablespoon marks printed on the wrapper. All you have to do is slice the butter where the line is.

Safety First!

A good cook never forgets that safety always comes first in the kitchen. Here are some important rules to follow.

Using knives, peelers, graters, and small kitchen appliances

- Never use a kitchen appliance or sharp utensil without asking an adult for help.

- Always use a cutting board when slicing or chopping ingredients. Grip the knife handle firmly, holding it so that the sharp edge is facing downward. Then slice through the ingredient, moving the knife away from yourself.

- After slicing raw meat or fish, wash the knife (with adult help) as well as the cutting board. You should also wash your hands with water and soap for at least twenty seconds before working with other ingredients.

- If you drop a knife, don't try to catch it. Instead, quickly step back and let the knife fall to the countertop or floor before picking it up by the handle.

- When using a vegetable peeler, press the edge of the blade into the vegetable's skin and then push the peeler away from yourself. Keep in mind that the more pressure you use, the thicker the peeling will be.

- Use electrical appliances, such as mixers and blenders, in a cleared space far away from the sink and other wet areas. And always unplug a mixer or blender before scraping a mixture from the beaters or blades.

Working around hot things

- Always ask an adult for help around a hot stovetop or oven.

- Make sure to point the handle of a stovetop pan away from you so you won't knock into it and accidentally tip the pot over.

- Use pot holders every time you touch a stovetop pot or skillet—even if it's just the lid. You should also use pot holders whenever you put a pan in the oven or take it out.

- Remember, steam can burn! Be sure to step back a bit when straining hot foods, such as pasta or cooked vegetables.

- Don't forget to shut off the oven or stove burner when the food is done baking or cooking.

Preparing Fruits and Vegetables

It's important to wash produce before adding it to a recipe. Here are some tips for making sure fruits and vegetables are clean and ready to use.

- Rinse produce well under plain running water. Don't use soap! If the produce is firm, like an apple or carrot, rub the surface to help remove any garden soil or grit. You can put softer fruits and vegetables, such as berries and broccoli florets, in a small colander or strainer before rinsing.

- Use a vegetable brush to scrub vegetables that grow underground, like potatoes and carrots. You should also scrub any fruits and vegetables that grow right on the ground, such as cucumbers and melons.

- Dry washed produce with a paper towel or reusable cleaning cloth and cut off any bruised parts before using it in a recipe.

Cleaning Up

A good cook always leaves the kitchen as tidy as they found it. This means cleaning all the bowls, pots, pans, and utensils you used to prepare the recipe. Here are some tips for making sure everything is spick-and-span.

- Always ask an adult for help washing knives and appliances with sharp blades, such as a blender or food processor.

- As you cook, try to give each bowl and utensil a quick rinse as soon as you're done with it. That way leftover food or batter won't stick to it before you can wash it with soap and water.

- Put all the ingredients back where they belong so you'll know just where to find them the next time you cook.

- Wipe down your work area—including the countertop and sink—with a damp paper towel or reusable cleaning cloth.

- Double-check that all the appliances you used are turned off before you leave the kitchen.

- Hang up your apron, or put it in the laundry if it needs to be washed.

Breakfast

Egg in a Nest

While she was working hard to save money for her restaurant, Tiana often woke up early with the sun! Here's a fun-to-cook breakfast that's as sunny as the South—an egg fried right inside a slice of toast.

Directions

1. Crack the egg by striking it against the rim of a bowl. Hold the shell above the bowl and carefully pull it apart. Pick out any shell fragments that may have fallen into the bowl along with the egg.

2. Use a 3-inch cookie cutter to cut a shape out of the center of the bread slice.

3. Melt the butter in a frying pan over medium heat. Place the bread in the pan and fry it lightly on one side for 1 to 2 minutes. You can also fry the cutout shape. Use a spatula to flip the bread over. Reduce the heat to low.

4. Carefully pour the egg into the cutout hole. Cover the pan and cook until the egg has set in the bread "nest," about 3 minutes. For an over-easy egg, flip the bread and egg, and cook it for another minute or so. Transfer it to a plate with the spatula.

Serves 1

Ingredients

1 egg

1 slice bread

1 Tbsp butter

Tip

For a fun "nest," use a cookie cutter shaped like a heart, a star, or a flower instead of a round one.

Ingredients

Unsalted butter,
for greasing

1 Tbsp olive oil

6 oz smoked mild
andouille sausage,
sliced into half-moons

3 cups baby spinach,
roughly chopped

6 Tbsp shredded sharp
cheddar

8 large eggs

½ cup half-and-half

½ tsp salt

¼ tsp pepper

Tip

*This recipe works best
using ramekins—small
round or oval baking
dishes that are oven safe.
They're fun to serve
dishes in, too!*

Big Easy Mini Frittatas

These little egg casseroles would make a fitting real-life brunch for one of Charlotte and Tiana's many make-believe-filled playdates. Along with spinach and cheese, each is filled with a spicy smoked sausage called andouille for a bit of Cajun flavor.

Directions

1. Heat the oven to 400°F and butter four 4-inch ramekins or similar baking dishes. Ask an adult for help at the stove. Warm the oil in a large skillet over medium heat. Add the sausage and cook, stirring frequently, until browned around the edges, about 5 minutes. Add the spinach and cook until wilted, about 2 minutes.

2. Evenly divide the sausage and spinach among the prepared ramekins and sprinkle each with one-fourth of the cheddar. In a small bowl, whisk together the eggs, salt, and pepper. Evenly divide the mixture among the ramekins.

3. Place the ramekins on a baking sheet. Ask an adult for help with the oven. Bake until the egg is set, about 25 minutes. Serve immediately.

Cheesy Grits

Corn grits are a Southern favorite you can enjoy for breakfast and beyond—and shredded sharp cheddar cheese can give them irresistible flavor. To make the grits extra creamy, add milk to the simmering liquid, just as Tiana's daddy, James, might have when he cooked them for her.

Directions

1. Ask an adult to help you at the stove. Bring the milk and 2½ cups water to a boil in a large saucepan. Stir in the grits until smooth, then cover, reduce to a simmer, and continue to cook, stirring occasionally, until the grits are creamy and thickened, about 15 minutes.

2. Remove the pan from the heat. Stir in the butter and cheddar until both are melted. Season with salt and pepper. Serve immediately.

Serves 4

Ingredients

¾ cup plus 2 Tbsp milk

¾ cup corn grits

2 Tbsp butter

⅔ cup shredded sharp cheddar

Salt and pepper to taste

Tip

These grits pair wonderfully with a side of toast.

Ingredients

1 medium green apple

2 large pieces whole wheat bread, toasted

¼ cup nut or seed butter

3 green grapes, halved lengthwise

4 large blueberries

1 strawberry, thinly sliced

Tip

Check out page 130 *for step-by-step photos on how to create this fun frog shape!*

Fruity Froggy Toast

Whether you're a prince, princess, or a royal of your own designation, you can customize this adorable fruit and nut-butter toast however you wish. A combination of apples, berries, and sunflower seed spread is particularly delicious, but the possibilities are truly endless!

Directions

1. Cut two rounded sides from the apple. With help from an adult, use a paring knife to carve a mouth into the center of each. Set aside. Trim the two remaining sides of the apple. Trim away 1 inch from the end of each and halve them lengthwise, as shown.

2. Spread 2 tablespoons of the nut or seed butter onto each slice of bread. Place a large apple piece on top for the mouth, then press two apple slice legs into place, as shown. Trim the ends of 4 of the grape halves and add them for the eyes. Use a dot of nut butter to attach a blueberry pupil to each.

3. Halve the remaining grape pieces. Add them to each frog for the feet. Finish with a strawberry slice tongue. Eat immediately.

Spicy Potato Hash

Over the years, Tiana has learned tricks for how to cook ingredients just right. And you won't find any undercooked potatoes in this hash thanks to one such trick: heating the potatoes in the microwave so they become tender more quickly once they hit your skillet.

Directions

1. In a large microwave-safe bowl, toss together the potatoes, ¾ teaspoon salt, and 1 tablespoon olive oil. Microwave, covered, on high until the potatoes start to become tender, stirring halfway through, about 5 minutes. Set aside.

2. Ask an adult for help at the stove. Warm the remaining tablespoon olive oil in a large nonstick skillet over medium heat. Add the onions and peppers and cook until beginning to soften, about 5 minutes. Add the garlic and cook 1 minute. Stir in the Creole seasoning, smoked paprika, and remaining ½ teaspoon salt, then add the potatoes. Cook 5 minutes without stirring to brown the potatoes on one side, then give the hash a stir. Continue to cook in this manner, letting the hash cook a few minutes, then stirring, until the potatoes are cooked through and nicely browned, about 15 minutes more.

3. Melt 1 tablespoon butter in a small nonstick skillet. Crack 2 of the eggs in the pan and cook until the whites are no longer translucent, about 3 to 4 minutes. Transfer each to a plate, season with salt and pepper, and then repeat with the remaining butter and eggs.

4. To serve, nestle a few generous spoonfuls of hash beneath each egg. Garnish with scallions if you'd like.

Serves 4

Ingredients

3 medium russet potatoes, cut into ½-inch cubes (about 6 cups)

1¼ tsp salt

2 Tbsp olive oil

1 large onion, sliced

1 large red bell pepper, diced

3 garlic cloves, diced

1 tsp Creole seasoning, such as Tony Chachere's

1 tsp smoked paprika

2 Tbsp butter

4 large eggs

Salt and pepper to taste

Chopped scallions, for garnish (optional)

Ingredients

Small (10-oz) loaf
of French bread, pulled
apart into 1-inch pieces

⅓ cup brown sugar

¾ tsp cinnamon

Dash of salt

6 large eggs

1¼ cups milk

1 tsp vanilla extract

Tip

*To change it up,
try using a loaf of
raisin bread instead
of French bread.*

Baked Caramel French Toast

This sweet French toast dish makes enough for a big group to enjoy! Share this with family and friends, and you'll feel like you're dining out together at Tiana's Palace.

Directions

1. Generously butter a 9 × 13-inch casserole dish. Place the bread pieces in the dish.

2. In a small bowl, mix together the brown sugar, cinnamon, and salt. Sprinkle the mixture over the bread.

3. In a mixing bowl, whisk together the eggs, milk, and vanilla extract. Pour the egg mixture evenly over the bread. Then use a spatula to press the bread down to make sure it is well coated.

4. Cover the baking pan with aluminum foil and refrigerate it for at least 4 hours, or overnight.

5. When you're ready to cook the French toast, heat the oven to 350°F. Ask an adult to help you with the oven. Bake the French toast with the foil in place for 20 minutes. Remove the foil, and continue baking for another 25 minutes.

6. Take the tray out of the oven and let cool for about 5 minutes before serving.

Banana French Toast

Craving a fruity French toast? This twist on the dish features sliced bananas—and it only takes a few minutes to cook.

Directions

1. First, cut a wide, deep slit down through the top crust of each bread slice. Stuff each pocket with 3 to 4 banana slices.

2. In a shallow dish or pie plate, whisk together the eggs and milk.

3. Heat the butter and oil in a large skillet over medium-high heat. Dip each bread slice in the egg mixture, turning it to coat both sides, and place it in the skillet.

4. Cook the French toast for 2 to 3 minutes on the first side until golden brown. Then use a spatula to flip the slices, and cook them for another 2 to 3 minutes. Serve with butter and maple syrup if you'd like.

Serves 6

Ingredients

1 (1-lb) loaf French or Italian bread, cut into thick slices

1 to 2 bananas, sliced

3 eggs

½ cup milk

1 to 2 Tbsp butter

1 to 2 Tbsp cooking oil of choice

Butter and maple syrup, for serving (optional)

Tip

Experiment by making this recipe with other types of fruit, like strawberries and blueberries.

Lunch

Serves 4

Ingredients

Muffuletta Spread

1 (5-oz) jar pimiento-stuffed green olives, drained and sliced

1 tomato, seeded and chopped

1 clove garlic, minced

1 tsp dried oregano

3 Tbsp olive oil

2 Tbsp balsamic vinegar

½ tsp ground black pepper

Sandwich

1 (9-inch) round loaf of Italian bread

Olive oil

¼ lb each of sliced baked ham, salami, provolone cheese, and Monterey Jack or Swiss cheese

Muffuletta Sandwich

Spread with garlicky chopped olives, this sandwich is popular in New Orleans, especially during the festive celebration of Mardi Gras.

Directions

1. Combine all the muffuletta spread ingredients in a bowl and stir until well mixed.

2. Slice the bread loaf in half lengthwise. Brush or drizzle the bottom piece with olive oil.

3. Layer on the meats, the cheeses, and the muffuletta spread, and then cover everything with the top half of the bread loaf.

4. Slice the sandwich into thick wedges.

Po'boy Sandwich

This sandwich is traditionally made with roast beef and gravy, but you can substitute just about any lunch meat you like. If you want to eat like a New Orleans native, create a "dressed" sandwich by adding lettuce, tomato, and mayonnaise.

Directions

1. Slice the roll or bread in half lengthwise and lightly toast both halves.

2. Spread mayonnaise on the bottom half of the roll. Layer on shredded lettuce, sliced tomatoes, and plenty of roast beef. Then spoon gravy on top of the roast beef.

3. Cover the sandwich with the top half of the roll and serve immediately.

Serves 1

Ingredients

French roll or large hunk of French bread

Mayonnaise

Shredded lettuce

Tomato slices

Sliced roast beef

¼ to ½ cup warm beef gravy

Makes 8 to 12

Ingredients

¼ cup mayonnaise

¼ tsp garlic powder

¼ tsp paprika

1 loaf each of
white bread and
wheat bread (1 slice
of each per sandwich)

Sliced ham

Sliced cheese

Tip

*You can make any
sandwich shape
you want by using
different cookie cutters.*

Ham and Cheese Blossom Sandwiches

Living near the Louisiana bayou, Tiana and her family are never too far from the great outdoors. Bring a bit of nature to lunchtime with these flower-shaped sandwiches made with ham, cheese, and a delicious spread.

Directions

1. In a small bowl, stir together the mayonnaise, garlic powder, and paprika.

2. For each sandwich, use a large flower-shaped cookie cutter (about 3 inches wide) to cut the center from a slice of white bread. Next, cut a matching flower shape from a slice of wheat bread.

3. Use a small round cookie cutter (about 1¼ inches wide) to cut a hole in the middle of each bread flower cutout. Place the center of the wheat flower into the white flower and the center of the white flower into the wheat flower.

4. Cut flower shapes from slices of ham and cheese (but don't cut holes in the centers).

5. Spread mayonnaise mixture on one of the bread flowers, and layer on the ham and cheese cutouts. Top off the sandwich with the second bread flower. You can spread a little more mayonnaise on this layer, too, if you'd like.

PB and J Blossom Sandwiches

Try out a sweeter twist on flower-shaped sandwiches with this peanut butter and jelly version.

Directions

1. For each sandwich, use a large flower-shaped cookie cutter (about 3 inches wide) to cut the center from a slice of bread.

2. Use a small round cookie cutter to cut a hole in the middle of half of the bread flower cutouts.

3. Spread the peanut butter and jelly on the whole flower shape. Then place the slice with the center hole on top.

Makes 8 to 12

Ingredients

1 loaf of white or wheat bread (2 slices of bread per sandwich)

Peanut butter

Jelly

Tip

Try pairing up different types of nut butters and jellies for this recipe and see which combos you like best.

Makes 6

Ingredients

Catfish

¼ cup flour

1 cup cornmeal

2 tsp Cajun seasoning

2 eggs, whisked

1 tsp salt

½ tsp pepper

1 to 1¼ lb catfish
(about 2 large fillets),
cut into 6 portions

Cooking spray

6 sandwich buns, toasted,
for serving

Tartar sauce, for serving

Slaw

3 cups slaw mix

2 Tbsp white vinegar

1 tsp sugar

Salt to taste

Oven-Baked Catfish Sandwich

A crunchy cornmeal coating makes the fish in these sandwiches just as tasty as a deep-fried version. Enjoy this dish as a family affair—just like Tiana, Eudora, and James—by letting everyone pitch in to prepare (and eat!) it.

Directions

1. Heat the oven to 450°F and line a baking sheet with parchment paper. In a shallow baking dish, combine the flour, cornmeal, salt, and Cajun seasoning. In another dish, whisk together the eggs, salt, and pepper.

2. To coat each piece of fish, dredge it in the egg mixture, then cover it with the cornmeal and place it on the prepared baking sheet. Repeat with the remaining fish, spacing the pieces 1 inch apart.

3. Coat the top of the fish with cooking spray. Ask an adult for help with the oven. Bake the fish 10 minutes, flip, and then coat the fish with cooking spray once more and return to the oven. Bake until the coating is golden and crisp, about 10 minutes more.

4. While the fish is baking, make the slaw. In a medium bowl, stir together the slaw mix, vinegar, and sugar. Season to taste with salt. To serve, place a piece of fish on the bottom half of a bun and top with slaw. Spread the tartar sauce on the top bun, then use it to sandwich the fish.

Sweet Dough Turnovers

Tiana loves discovering her friends' favorite foods. These turnovers are perfect for sharing with all sorts of eaters—you can try them with the more traditional sweet potato filling, or a broccoli and cheese filling, or create your own custom versions.

Directions

1. In a small bowl, whisk together the flour, baking powder, and salt, and set aside.

2. Using a handheld mixer, cream together the butter and sugar until the mixture is light and fluffy, about 3 minutes. Add the vanilla and the egg and mix to combine. Alternate mixing in a little of the flour mixture with a little of the milk until both are combined. Transfer the dough to a sheet of plastic wrap, roll it up, and place it in the refrigerator for 15 minutes.

3. Preheat the oven to 375°F. Combine the ingredients for your preferred filling in a small bowl. Remove the dough from the refrigerator and separate into 4 pieces. On a floured surface, roll the dough out into 4 circles with a rolling pin. You can use the mouth of a small bowl to cut out perfect circles, or leave them as they are for a more homemade look.

4. Using a spoon, scoop a fourth of the filling into the center of each small circle. Add water to the edges of the dough, fold the circle in half, and crimp the edges together with a fork.

5. Ask an adult for help with the oven. Place on a baking sheet, and bake for 12 to 15 minutes or until golden brown on the outside. Once the turnovers are done, make sure to let them cool down before taking a bite!

Makes 4

Ingredients

Sweet Dough

1 cup plus 2 Tbsp flour

½ tsp baking powder

¼ tsp salt

3 Tbsp unsalted butter, softened

1 Tbsp sugar

¼ tsp vanilla extract

1 Tbsp beaten egg

2 Tbsp milk

Sweet Potato Filling

1 (15-oz) can yams in syrup, drained and mashed

¼ tsp cinnamon

¼ tsp nutmeg

¼ tsp ginger

Broccoli and Cheese Filling

1 cup broccoli, cooked

½ cup cheddar cheese, shredded

1 cup cooked chicken or ham, cubed (optional)

Ingredients

2 large flatbreads

¼ cup pizza sauce

¾ cup shredded
mozzarella

1 small red bell pepper

1 small yellow bell pepper

1 small green bell pepper

Mini pepperoni

Tip

*You can also assemble
this recipe with
traditional pizza dough
if you prefer.*

Princess Flatbread Pizza

**While these crowns are for eating rather than wearing,
their culinary creativity can still be appreciated by any royal.
The recipe calls for flatbread since it's easier to cut and holds
its shape while it bakes.**

Directions

1. Heat the oven to 425°F. Use kitchen shears to cut each
   flatbread into two crown shapes, as shown. Arrange them on
   a baking sheet 2 inches apart. Spread a thin layer of pizza
   sauce onto each crown, leaving a ½-inch border. Cover with
   mozzarella.

2. Use a paring knife or mini food cutters to shape several pieces
   from each bell peppers. Arrange them on each crown as desired,
   along with mini pepperoni.

3. Ask an adult for help with the oven.
   Bake the pizzas until the
   cheese is melted and
   bubbly and the bread is
   golden and crisp, about
   10 minutes.
   Serve immediately.

Dinner

Chicken and Sausage Gumbo

Makes 4

As a little girl, Tiana loved making gumbo with her daddy, James—and the whole neighborhood came rushing over whenever they made a pot! Bring your family together with this take on gumbo. To make it, you start by cooking a roux—a mixture of oil and flour—which adds color and richness to the dish.

Directions

1. Ask an adult for help at the stove. In a large, heavy skillet, warm ¼ cup of the oil over medium heat. Add the flour and cook, stirring continuously, until the mixture is a deep chocolate color, about 15 minutes. Transfer to a heat-proof bowl.

2. In a large pot, heat 1 tablespoon oil. Add the sausage and cook until well browned, about 6 minutes. Transfer to a plate. Add the remaining tablespoon oil, along with the onion, bell pepper, and celery, and cook until softened, about 5 minutes. Add the garlic and cook 1 minute more. Stir in the salt, pepper, thyme, and bay leaves.

3. Add the chicken stock and bring the mixture to a simmer. Add the roux (the flour and oil mixture) and whisk until smooth. Add the chicken and cook, stirring occasionally, until the chicken is cooked through and the flavors meld, about 20 minutes. To serve, scoop a generous portion of rice into a bowl, then ladle the gumbo on top.

Ingredients

¼ cup plus 2 Tbsp vegetable oil

¼ cup flour

12 oz mild andouille sausage, sliced

1 large onion, chopped

1 large green bell pepper, chopped

2 stalks celery, chopped

2 garlic cloves, minced

1½ tsp salt

½ tsp pepper

¾ tsp dried thyme

2 small bay leaves

6 cups chicken stock

½ lb boneless chicken breast, diced

Cooked white rice, for serving

Tip

Be sure to use a heavy-bottom pot for this recipe, and keep close watch as the ingredients brown so they don't burn.

Ingredients

4 Tbsp flour

3 Tbsp vegetable oil, divided

1 large onion, diced

2 Tbsp Cajun seasoning

2 andouille chicken sausages, thinly sliced

2 bell peppers, diced

2 to 3 celery stalks, diced

2 carrots, diced

3½ cups vegetable or chicken stock

½ lb shrimp, any size

1 medium potato, cooked and mashed

Salt to taste

2 Tbsp minced fresh parsley

12 whole wheat rolls

Tip

These are extra fun to eat with your hands! Pay special attention when prepping the rolls so they're easy to hold.

Gumbo Rolls

Tiana continues to put new spins on the dishes her daddy taught her as a little girl. Try a fun and unique twist on gumbo with this recipe—gumbo served in a roll! Much like in the first gumbo recipe, you'll start this one by creating a roux.

Directions

1. Ask an adult for help at the stove. To make the roux, in a small saucepan over medium-low heat, whisk together the flour and 2 tablespoons of the oil. Cook very slowly until the roux is dark brown, about 40 minutes, whisking or stirring frequently. Set aside.

2. To make the gumbo, heat the remaining tablespoon oil in a large pot over medium-high heat. Add the onion, Cajun seasoning, and sausages and sauté for 5 minutes. Add the bell pepper, celery, and carrots, and sauté 5 minutes more. Then add the stock and the roux. Bring to a boil, then reduce heat and simmer, covered, until vegetables are barely soft, about 15 minutes. Add the shrimp to the pot, stir to incorporate, and cook, covered, 5 minutes more. Add the mashed potato, then taste for salt. The amount you need will depend heavily on how salty your stock or broth is. Set aside to cool.

3. To prepare the rolls, ask an adult to help you use an apple corer or a knife to cut out the center of each one. You want to leave enough bread around the edges that the stew won't be able to soak through.

4. To assemble, spoon gumbo into the rolls just until peeking out from the top. Reserve remaining gumbo for eating later.

Diner-Style Chicken and Biscuits

Comfort food was always on the menu at Cal's Diner, where Tiana got one of her first jobs. This dish makes for a wonderfully homey dinner!

Directions

1. Melt the butter for the filling over medium heat in a large ovenproof pot. Stir in the onion and celery. Put a lid on the pan and cook for 7 to 8 minutes, stirring occasionally. Then stir in the flour.

2. Whisk the broth into the pan. When it starts to thicken, whisk in the milk. Add the sage, thyme, chicken, and peas, carrots, and/or corn. Continue cooking and stirring for 5 to 7 minutes. Add salt and pepper to taste

3. Remove the pan from the stovetop and heat the oven to 375° F. Meanwhile, make the biscuit topping by combining the flour, baking powder, and salt in a bowl. Use your fingertips to rub in the butter. Pour in the milk and stir just until the dough pulls together.

4. Turn the dough onto a floured surface and knead it 2 or 3 times with floured hands. Pat the dough into a ½-inch-thick disk. Using a small cookie cutter, cut out dough circles and place as many as will fit, barely touching, on the filling.

5. Ask an adult to help you with the oven. Bake until the biscuits brown and the filling bubbles, about 20 to 30 minutes. Let it cool for 10 minutes before serving.

Serves 6 to 8

Ingredients

4 Tbsp butter

1 cup onion, chopped

1 stalk celery, chopped

⅓ cup flour

1½ cups chicken broth

1½ cups milk

½ tsp each of dried sage and dried thyme

2½ cups cooked chicken, diced

2 cups cooked peas, chopped carrots, or corn (or a mix of these)

Salt and pepper to taste

Biscuit Topping

2 cups flour

1 Tbsp baking powder

½ tsp salt

¼ cup cold butter, cut into ¼-inch pieces

¾ cup milk

Tip

You can use frozen or fresh veggies for this recipe!

Ingredients

Cooking oil of choice
for the baking pan

4 Tbsp butter

⅔ cup buttery
crackers, crushed

¼ cup grated
Parmesan cheese

½ tsp dried basil

½ tsp dried oregano

¼ tsp garlic powder

1 lb sole, scrod, perch,
or other mild fish fillets

Tip

*Try dipping these
fillets into ketchup
or tartar sauce!*

Short-Order Fish Fillets

When Tiana worked at Duke's Café, the cook Buford's specialty was whipping up delicious food fast! This breaded fish would fit right in on the menu.

Directions

1. Heat the oven to 350°F. Grease a 9 × 13–inch baking pan and set it aside.

2. Melt the butter in a saucepan over low heat. Then pour it into a mixing bowl. In a pie pan, stir together the crushed crackers, grated cheese, basil, oregano, and garlic powder.

3. Place the fish fillets in the melted butter. Turn the fillets over so that both sides are coated. One at a time, dip the fish fillets in the crumb mixture, again coating both sides, and place them in the baking pan.

4. Bake the fish until it flakes apart when you insert a fork, about 20 to 25 minutes.

Jammin' Jambalaya

Like many Cajun and Creole recipes, jambalaya is a delicious mix of seasoned meats and vegetables. One of the things that makes jambalaya different is that you stir uncooked rice right into the pot to simmer in the flavorful liquid.

Directions

1. Ask an adult to help you with the stove. Heat the oil in a large frying pan or pot over medium-high heat. Sauté the chicken until cooked through, about 5 minutes. Reduce the heat to medium.

2. Stir in the sausage, onion, celery, bell pepper, and garlic. Sprinkle on the salt and ground black pepper, and stir again. Cook the mixture for 5 minutes, stirring occasionally.

3. Stir in the chopped tomatoes and the uncooked rice. Then stir in the chicken broth. Bring the mixture to a boil.

4. Reduce the heat to low and cover the pan. Simmer the jambalaya until the rice is tender, about 20 minutes. Stir in the Worcestershire and hot pepper sauces.

Serves 6 to 8

Ingredients

2 Tbsp olive oil

2 boneless, skinless chicken breasts, cut into 1-inch chunks

½ pound andouille sausage, cooked and thinly sliced

1 medium onion, chopped

2 large celery stalks, chopped

1 small bell pepper, seeded and chopped

2 cloves garlic, peeled and chopped

¼ tsp salt

⅛ tsp ground black pepper

1 cup canned chopped tomatoes, undrained

2 cups uncooked white rice

4 cups chicken broth

2 tsp Worcestershire sauce

1 tsp hot pepper sauce

Tip

If you like your food on the mild side, add less Worcestershire sauce and hot pepper sauce than the recipe calls for.

Ingredients

2 Tbsp olive oil

1 medium onion, chopped

1 large celery stalk, chopped

1 small bell pepper, seeded and chopped

3 scallions, chopped

2 Tbsp chopped parsley

2 (15-oz) cans kidney beans with the juice

1 (14½-oz) can chopped tomatoes

½ lb andouille sausage, cooked and thinly sliced

4 slices bacon, cooked and crumbled

1½ tsp Worcestershire sauce

¼ tsp cayenne pepper

3 cups cooked white rice

Tip

This dish can be spicy, so be careful not to overseason with the cayenne pepper!

Red Beans and Rice

Flavored with crumbled bacon and sausage left over from Sunday dinner, this traditional Louisiana dish has long been a popular Monday special at New Orleans restaurants—so it would fit right in on the Tiana's Palace menu.

Directions

1. Ask an adult to help you at the stove. Heat the oil in a large frying pan over medium heat. Add the onion, celery, bell pepper, scallions, and parsley to the pan and sauté them for 4 to 5 minutes, stirring occasionally.

2. Add the beans, tomatoes, sausage, bacon, Worcestershire sauce, and cayenne pepper to the vegetables, and stir until the ingredients are evenly mixed. Cover the pan and simmer the mixture for 30 minutes, stirring occasionally.

3. Serve the beans over white rice.

Musical Meatloaf

Louis and the Firefly Five can't make music on empty stomachs! This hearty meatloaf is a showstopper, just like Louis's trumpet playing.

Directions

1. Heat the oven to 350°F. Grease the bottom and sides of a 2½-quart casserole dish.

2. Combine the ground beef or turkey and ground pork in a large mixing bowl.

3. In a small bowl or cup, stir together the celery salt, garlic powder, thyme, paprika, and pepper. Sprinkle the mixture over the meat.

4. Add the bread crumbs, onion, ketchup, milk, and eggs to the meat. Use a wooden spoon to stir all the ingredients together until they are well mixed. Pack the meatloaf mixture into the casserole dish.

5. Ask an adult to help you with the oven. Place the meatloaf in the oven and bake for 50 minutes. Then carefully remove it from the oven. Spread the ketchup and honey mixture on top using a spoon or spatula. Return the meatloaf to the oven to bake for 10 more minutes.

6. Let the meatloaf cool for a few minutes before you slice and serve it.

Serves 6 to 8

Ingredients

1 lb ground beef
or turkey
(85% to 90% lean)

1 lb ground pork

1 tsp celery salt

1 tsp garlic powder

1 tsp dried thyme

1 tsp paprika

¼ tsp pepper

1 cup bread crumbs

½ cup onion, minced

½ cup ketchup

½ cup milk

2 large eggs, lightly beaten

Topping
½ cup ketchup with
1 Tbsp honey stirred in

Tip

Leftover meatloaf tastes great in a sandwich, especially if you toast the bread.

Serves 6 to 8

Ingredients

½ lb dried black-eyed peas

1 Tbsp butter

½ lb baked ham, cubed

1 medium onion, chopped

2 stalks celery, chopped

2 medium carrots, chopped

2 cloves garlic, minced

¼ tsp celery salt

¼ tsp red pepper flakes

Dash of pepper

1 cup long-grain white rice

Tip

When you rinse the black-eyed peas, be sure to sort through them for any loose pebbles that might have been mixed in by mistake when they were picked.

Hoppin' John

Tiana puts food on her restaurant menu that can be enjoyed year-round. But sometimes, dishes can make holidays extra special! This popular Southern dish is supposed to bring good luck if you eat it on New Year's Day.

Directions

1. Rinse the black-eyed peas in a metal strainer, then put them in a large saucepan.

2. Ask an adult for help at the stove. Pour in 4 cups of water. Bring the black-eyed peas to a boil and cook them for 2 minutes. Then remove the pan from the heat and let the black-eyed peas stand for 1 hour.

3. Melt the butter in a large skillet over low heat. Add the ham, onion, celery, carrots, garlic, celery salt, red pepper flakes, and pepper. Cook the mixture until it heats through and the onion starts to look clear (about 6 to 8 minutes).

4. Add the black-eyed peas and their liquid to the skillet and stir. Bring the mixture to a boil, and then lower the heat until the cooking slows down to a simmer. Cover the pan and continue cooking until the beans are tender, about 6 to 8 minutes.

5. Pour in 1 more cup of water, and stir in the rice. Re-cover the skillet and continue simmering for about 20 minutes, or until the rice is cooked.

6. Drain off any extra liquid, give the Hoppin' John a final stir, and serve.

Snake Stew

Mama Odie and Juju the snake make for a dynamic duo—and so do these snake-shaped breadsticks and stew! Beware of the spicy bite from the chorizo. . . .

Directions

1. Heat the oven to 400°F and line two baking sheets with parchment paper. Divide the dough into 8 to 10 portions. On a lightly floured surface, roll a portion into a 2-foot-long rope. Working directly on one of the prepared sheets, wind and shape the rope into a snake. Repeat with the remaining dough, spacing them 2 inches apart.

2. Press a pair of peppercorn eyes into each snake. Ask an adult for help with the oven. Bake the snakes until golden and puffed, about 10 minutes. Set aside to cool.

3. Ask an adult for help at the stove. In a large pot over medium heat, warm the oil. Add the chorizo and cook until browned, about 8 minutes. Transfer the meat to a bowl. Add the onion to the pan and cook until softened, about 3 minutes. Add the garlic and cook 1 minute. Season with the salt and pepper, then add the broth and 3 cups water, and bring to a boil.

4. Place the potatoes in the pot and reduce the heat to a simmer. Continue to simmer until the potatoes are cooked through, about 12 minutes. Remove half the stew from the pot and puree. Add it back to the pot along with the kale and white beans, and return to a simmer. Cook until the kale is wilted, about 8 minutes. Serve each portion hot in a bowl topped with a snake breadstick.

Serves 6

Ingredients

Breadsticks

¾ to 1 lb pizza dough

Flour, for dusting

1 Tbsp peppercorns

Stew

2 Tbsp olive oil

1 (14-oz) package chorizo, thinly sliced

1 large onion, chopped

3 garlic cloves, minced

1½ tsp salt

¼ tsp pepper

4 cups chicken broth

3 medium Yukon Gold potatoes, peeled and cut into 1-inch cubes

½ large bunch green kale, torn into bite-size pieces (about 6 cups)

1 (14-oz) can white beans, rinsed and drained

Serves 6 to 8

Ingredients

1 lb elbow macaroni, cooked according to the package directions

Butter for greasing the baking pan

3 cups half-and-half or whole milk

12 to 18 slices total, American or cheddar cheese

12 buttery crackers

Salt, pepper, and paprika to taste

Tip

Make this recipe your own by adding different types of cheese or crackers.

Enchanting Macaroni and Cheese

Layered with cheese and sprinkled with buttery cracker crumbs, this dish is so tasty that you'll be spellbound!

Directions

1. Heat the oven to 350°F. Grease a 13 × 9–inch baking pan or large casserole dish.

2. Spoon a third of the cooked macaroni into the pan. Pour in 1 cup of the half-and-half or milk. Then cover everything with 4 to 6 slices of the cheese. Add two more layers of pasta, half-and-half or milk, and cheese.

3. Place the crackers in a sealable plastic bag and crush them with your fingers or a rolling pin. Add the salt, pepper, and paprika to the cracker crumbs. Sprinkle the crumbs on top of the pasta and cheese. Bake until bubbly, about 35 to 45 minutes.

Sides

Skillet Cornbread

This slightly sweetened quick bread is a cinch to whip up, and there's hardly a Southern supper it doesn't go well with.

Directions

1. Heat the oven to 400°F. Use a pat of the butter to grease a 10-inch cast-iron skillet (or a 10-inch deep-dish pie pan). Ask an adult to help you at the stove. Melt the remaining butter in a small saucepan over low heat. Remove the pan from the stove and set it aside.

2. Sift the flour, cornmeal, sugar, baking soda, baking powder, and salt into a large bowl. In a separate bowl, whisk together the eggs and buttermilk. Pour the melted butter into the buttermilk mixture.

3. Make a well in the dry ingredients and pour in the buttermilk mixture. Stir the batter just until evenly blended. Then pour it into the buttered skillet.

4. Ask an adult for help with the oven. Bake the cornbread until a toothpick inserted into the center comes out clean, about 25 to 30 minutes. Cool the bread in the pan on a wire rack for 10 minutes before slicing it.

Serves 8 to 10

Ingredients

3 Tbsp butter

1 cup flour

1 cup fine yellow cornmeal

2 Tbsp sugar

1 tsp baking soda

1 tsp baking powder

½ tsp salt

2 large eggs, lightly beaten

2 cups buttermilk

Tip

This cornbread makes a tasty breakfast. Trying serving it warm, with a side of butter and honey.

Serves 6 to 8

Ingredients

2 cups milk

1 cup water

1 Tbsp butter

1 tsp salt

1 cup cornmeal

2 eggs

2 Tbsp honey

2 ½ tsp baking powder

Tip

*Not sure how to
separate egg whites
and yolks?*
**Check out the
glossary on page 138!**

Southern Spoon Bread

If you love cornbread, then you should try spoon bread next!
It tastes similar, but it has a delicious gooey texture that's fun
to spoon up at mealtime.

Directions

1. Heat the oven to 375°F. Butter a 2-quart casserole dish.

2. Ask an adult to help you at the stove. Heat the milk and
   water in a large heavy saucepan over medium heat.
   Turn the heat to low as soon as bubbles form against the
   pan (before the milk boils). Add the butter and salt,
   and stir until the butter melts.

3. Slowly whisk the cornmeal into the milk.
   Keep whisking just until the mixture thickens
   (about 1 minute). Remove the pan from
   the heat and let the cornmeal cool a bit.

4. Separate the egg yolks and the egg
   whites into different mixing bowls.

5. Beat the egg whites with a mixer until
   they are foamy and stiff, and set them
   aside.

6. Beat together the yolks, honey, and baking
   powder with a fork or whisk. Then whisk
   the mixture into the cornmeal. Pour the
   cornmeal mixture into the bowl of beaten
   egg whites.

7. Use a rubber spatula to gently fold the
   egg whites into the cornmeal.

8. Scrape the spoon bread batter into the
   casserole dish. Ask an adult to help you
   put the dish in the oven. Bake it until
   the top turns golden brown and a
   toothpick inserted in the middle comes
   out clean (about 25 to 30 minutes).
   Serve the spoon bread warm, scooping it
   out of the casserole dish with a big spoon.

Naveen-Style Green Beans

Prince Naveen had no idea how to slice and dice vegetables—but with Tiana's help, he became an expert! Hone your own veggie prep skills with this delicious take on green beans.

Directions

1. Wash and trim the beans, then snap them in half. Place the beans in a saucepan with enough water to cover them. Ask an adult to help you at the stove. Bring the water to a boil, then reduce the heat and simmer the beans until just barely tender, about 8 minutes.

2. Drain the beans and immediately rinse them in cold water to stop the cooking process. Set them aside.

3. Sauté the mushrooms, onions, and garlic in the olive oil until tender, about 5 minutes. Add the water chestnuts, basil, Italian seasoning, and salt and pepper. Stir in the green beans and cook the mixture for 3 to 4 minutes to heat it through.

Serves 8

Ingredients

2 lb fresh green beans

1 cup sliced fresh mushrooms

½ cup diced onions

3 cloves garlic, minced

⅓ cup olive oil

1 (8-oz) can water chestnuts, drained

½ tsp dried basil

½ tsp Italian seasoning

Salt and pepper to taste

Tip

Garlic cloves are easier to peel and chop if you crush them with a rolling pin first.

Ingredients

2 cups green beans, sliced and cooked

1 (10-oz) can cream of mushroom soup

¼ cup milk

½ tsp salt

½ tsp pepper

1 tsp garlic powder

1⅓ cups french fried onions

1 cup cheddar cheese, shredded

Tip

This green bean casserole is the perfect dish to round out a big feast, like Thanksgiving or Christmas dinner.

Festive Green Bean Casserole

Put another delicious spin on green beans with this classic Southern vegetable dish—perfect for a holiday dinner, or year-round.

Directions

1. Preheat the oven to 350°F. In a large bowl, stir together the green beans, mushroom soup, milk, salt, pepper, garlic powder, and ⅔ cup of the french fried onions. Ask an adult to help you with the oven. Pour into a greased 1½-quart baking dish and bake for 15 minutes.

2. Add the cheddar cheese and the remaining ⅔ cup french fried onions, and bake for another 5 to 10 minutes or until the cheese is melted.

Confetti Corn

Made with red pepper, yellow corn, and green basil, this colorful medley is as fun-filled as a musical night at Tiana's Palace.

Directions

1. Ask an adult to help you at the stove. Heat the vegetable oil in a medium-size frying pan over medium-low heat. Sauté the diced red pepper in the oil for 2 minutes.

2. Add the corn, basil, butter, and bacon (if using). Stir the ingredients together, and cook them until they are hot and well mixed and the butter is melted.

3. Remove the pan from the heat. Stir in salt and pepper to taste.

Serves 6

Ingredients

1 tsp vegetable oil

½ cup diced
red bell pepper

2 cups cooked corn

1 tsp dried basil

½ tsp butter

Salt and pepper to taste

3 strips cooked
bacon, crumbled
(optional)

Tip

Leftover cooked sweet corn, cut off the cob, tastes especially good in this recipe.

Oven-Baked Potato Wedges

Serves 4

These chunky wedges are like french fries, but instead of being fried, they crisp up in the oven.

Ingredients

4 medium Idaho potatoes

¼ cup olive oil

Salt to taste

Directions

1. Heat the oven to 425°F. Peel the potatoes and slice them into about 10 wedges. Dry off any excess starch with paper towels.

2. In a baking dish, toss the potatoes with the oil to coat them. Ask an adult for help with the oven. Bake the potatoes for 25 minutes, turning them at least once. Sprinkle on salt.

Tip

You can also try this recipe with other types of potatoes, like sweet potatoes.

Transforming Fruit Salad

Dr. Facilier uses magic to stir up trouble, such as changing humans into frogs. But not all transformations require magic. With this recipe, for instance, all you need is fresh mint to turn a bowl of fruit into a fantastic salad.

Directions

1. Combine the melon, apple, grapes, and kiwis in a large mixing bowl. Toss the fruit with a wooden spoon to evenly distribute the pieces.

2. Chop all but 2 or 3 of the mint sprigs. Toss the chopped mint into the salad and use the remaining sprigs for garnish.

Serves 6

Ingredients

4 cups cantaloupe or other melon balls

1 apple, cored and thinly sliced

½ lb grapes, halved

2 kiwis, peeled, quartered, and sliced

⅓ cup fresh mint sprigs

Tip

Before chopping mint or other fresh herbs, rinse them well and pat them dry.

Snacks

Serves 5

Ingredients

Remoulade

¾ cup mayonnaise

2 Tbsp ketchup

1 Tbsp brown mustard

1½ tsp hot pepper sauce

2 tsp Worcestershire sauce

1 tsp prepared horseradish

4 tsp chopped parsley

4 tsp capers, finely chopped

1 tsp grated garlic

Juice and zest of ½ lemon

1 tsp salt

1¼ tsp Creole seasoning

1 Tbsp chives

Black pepper to taste

Shrimp

3 stalks celery, sliced

2 carrots, sliced

4 cloves garlic, smashed

2 sprigs fresh thyme

1 small lemon, halved

1 lb jumbo shrimp, shell on

Shrimp and Remoulade Sauce

The name remoulade might sound fancy, but it's a delicious zesty condiment that can be spread on sandwich and used as a dip! Serve it alongside shrimp for a tasty snack.

Directions

1. In a small bowl, whisk together all the ingredients for the remoulade. Taste and adjust seasoning as desired. Cover and set aside to let the flavors meld.

2. In a large pot, combine the celery, carrots, garlic, thyme, and half the lemon with 2 quarts water. Ask an adult for help at the stove. Bring to a boil.

3. Prepare an ice bath in a large bowl. Place the shrimp in the boiling water and let cook until pink, about 3 minutes. Transfer immediately to the ice bath, cool 5 minutes, then pat dry, arrange on a platter, and refrigerate until ready to serve. If you like, you can peel the shrimp before plating.

4. Squeeze the remaining lemon half over the shrimp and serve with the remoulade on the side.

Shrimp Dip

Just as Ray and the fireflies light up the night, this flavorful dip will light up your taste buds! This delicious dip is perfect to serve at parties.

Directions

1. Preheat the oven to 375°F and prepare a baking dish by lightly greasing the sides and bottom.

2. Combine all ingredients in a large bowl and mix well. Pour the mixture into the prepared baking dish.

3. Ask an adult for help with the oven. Bake for 18 to 20 minutes or until the mixture is slightly bubbly. Serve with crackers or baguette slices. Enjoy warm!

Serves 12

Ingredients

1 (12-oz) package frozen small salad shrimp, defrosted

2 to 3 green onions, sliced

1 red bell pepper, diced

¼ cup sour cream

1 cup light cream cheeses

¼ cup Parmesan cheese

1 cup shredded cheddar cheese

1 Tbsp lemon juice

Zest of 1 lemon

1 Tbsp Cajun seasoning

2 tsp Worcestershire sauce

Crackers or baguette slices for serving

Tip

Try dipping different types of crackers and bread into this dip and see which you like best.

Makes 12 muffins

Ingredients

1½ cups whole wheat flour

½ cup coconut sugar

1 tsp baking powder

½ tsp baking soda

½ tsp salt

1½ tsp pumpkin pie spice

2 cups sweet potatoes, cooked and mashed

¾ cup almond or oat milk

2 Tbsp maple syrup

1 Tbsp apple cider vinegar

½ tsp vanilla extract

Tip

If you don't have whole sweet potatoes on hand, you can use an equal quantity of the canned variety, provided the only ingredient is pureed sweet potatoes; sweet potatoes in syrup won't work for this.

Sweet Potato Pie Muffins

Sweet potato pie is a Southern classic. This recipe puts a healthier twist on sweet potato pie, reimagining the dish as muffins. They make for a filling afternoon snack.

Directions

1. Preheat the oven to 375°F. Grease or spray a 12-cup muffin pan with cooking spray.

2. In a large mixing bowl, combine the flour, coconut sugar, baking powder, baking soda, salt, and pumpkin pie spice. Whisk to combine. Make a space with the whisk in the center of the ingredients and add the sweet potatoes, milk, maple syrup, apple cider vinegar, and vanilla extract. Switching to a spatula, fold ingredients together until combined.

3. Divide the batter among the prepared muffin-pan cups. Ask an adult for help with the oven. Bake until golden, about 20 minutes.

Slithering Snake Snack

This tiny platter for one reimagines hummus and cucumbers as a fun slithering scene, inspired by Mama Odie's loyal companion Juju the snake. What's more, its short ingredient list and easy steps mean you can prep and enjoy in just minutes.

Directions

1. Evenly spread the hummus in the bottom of a small oval or round baking dish. Trim a 1½-inch length from one end of the cucumber. Cut a wedge from the piece to form the mouth, as shown. Set aside. Thinly slice the remaining cucumber, reserving one slice. Arrange the head and body slices in the hummus, as shown.

2. Use the end of a plastic straw to cut two eyes from the remaining cucumber slice. Use a small dot of the hummus (a toothpick works well for applying) to attach the eyes. Trim a tongue from the carrot and set it in place. Garnish with a few pieces of dill, as shown. Serve immediately.

Serves 1

Ingredients

¼ cup hummus

1 large Persian cucumber

1 orange baby carrot

2 sprigs fresh dill

Tip

Check out page 131 *for step-by-step photos on how to create this fun snake shape!*

Ingredients

2 cups shredded cheddar

2 oz cream cheese, softened

¼ cup plus 2 Tbsp mayonnaise

¼ cup plus 2 Tbsp finely chopped roasted red bell pepper

½ tsp salt

½ tsp pepper

4 stalks celery, cut into 2- to 3-inch lengths

6 large black olives

2 slices white cheddar

12 small green olives

3 chives, snipped into 1-inch lengths

12 yellow cherry tomatoes

Tip

Check out page 132 *for step-by-step photos on how to create the bugs' eyes and antennae!*

Pimento Cheese Bugs

Celery sticks stuffed with homemade pimento cheese are the base of these cute snacks made in the likeness of Ray and his firefly family. The recipe for the cheese is doubled, so you'll have plenty of extra to snack on with crackers, more veggies, or any way you wish. As Ray might say, *"Ça c'est bon!"*

Directions

1. In a large bowl, combine the shredded cheddar, cream cheese, mayonnaise, bell peppers, salt, and pepper. Blend at low speed until smooth with a hand mixer or in a stand mixer fitted with a paddle attachment. Set aside.

2. Use the end of a plastic straw to cut the black olives into 12 pairs of eyes. With a mini oval cutter, shape 12 ovals from the cheese slices and halve each for the wings. Use a toothpick to poke 2 holes in the side of each green olive, then slide a chive into each opening, as shown.

3. Fill the center of the celery sticks with pimento cheese. If you like, you can trim a small piece from the bottom of each celery piece so that it sits flat. Top each with a cherry tomato body and green olive head. Use a bit of the leftover pimento cheese to attach the black olive eyes, then finish by adding a pair of cheese wings to each. Refrigerate the celery snacks and any leftover pimento cheese until ready to serve.

Beverages

Berrylicious Bayou Smoothie

Whether you're going on adventures in a Louisiana swamp or lying low on a steamy summer day, this frosty fruit drink will help you keep your cool!

Directions

1. Measure all the ingredients into a blender and put the top on.
2. Ask an adult for help with the blender. Blend on the puree setting until smooth, about 30 seconds or so.

Serves 1

Ingredients

½ cup fresh orange juice

½ cup nonfat yogurt

¼ cup blueberries, washed

1 frozen banana

Tip

Chopping the banana into pieces before freezing it will make it easier to blend.

Ingredients

3 bags peppermint tea

1 quart near-boiling water

2 bags green tea

Maple syrup to taste

Ice

Tip

If you're feeling creative, you can try this recipe with other types of tea besides peppermint.

Minty Iced Tea

The summers can get hot, especially in a place like New Orleans! A hint of maple syrup is the secret to this old-time thirst quencher.

Directions

1. Steep the bags of peppermint tea in the water for 2 minutes. Add the bags of green tea and steep for 4 more minutes.

2. Remove the teabags and let the tea cool.

3. Stir in maple syrup to taste. Pour the tea into tall glasses filled with plenty of ice.

Juju Juleps

Even Mama Odie's pet snake, Juju, knows how nice a sweet drink is on a sultry day in the bayou. This one combines lemon juice with the fizz of ginger ale.

Directions

1. Combine the water, lemon juice, sugar, and mint sprigs in a medium-size glass bowl. Let the mixture steep for 30 minutes.

2. Strain the liquid into a serving pitcher. Pour in the ginger ale.

3. Serve the juleps over ice in tall glasses.

Serves 6 to 7

Ingredients

2 cups cold water

⅔ cup fresh lemon juice (about 2 lemons)

⅓ cup sugar

4 mint sprigs

1 qt ginger ale

Ingredients

1 lemon

3 cups blueberries,
plus more for garnish

1 (1-inch) piece fresh
ginger, sliced

1½ cups sugar

Plain seltzer or
sparkling water

Lemon zest for garnish
(optional)

Tip

*The outermost part
of a citrus rind
(also called zest)
can be used to add lots of
flavor to a recipe.
Here, it's used to make
the syrup taste lemony.
Don't know how to
remove zest?*
**Check out the glossary
on page 138
for instructions.**

Blueberry Sparkler

Just like Dr. Facilier, you can easily make your own homemade potion—but don't worry, there's nothing villainous about this tasty beverage. This bubbly violet-colored soda is refreshing and fun to drink.

Directions

1. Use a vegetable peeler to remove half the rind from the lemon. Ask an adult for help at the stove. Place the rind in a large saucepan, along with the blueberries, ginger, sugar, and 2 cups water. Bring to a boil, then reduce the heat to low and simmer 20 minutes. Let cool completely.

2. Strain the syrup into a clean jar. To make each sparkler, fill an 8-ounce glass with ice. Add 2 tablespoons syrup, then top off with seltzer or sparkling water. If you'd like, garnish with lemon zest and several fresh blueberries. Serve immediately.

Sweets

Tiana-Style Beignets

Makes 14 to 16

You know you're in New Orleans if the doughnuts are square and don't have holes. These pillow-shaped French pastries are called beignets, and even before she opened Tiana's Palace, Tiana was known for making the very best!

Ingredients

3 cups flour

⅓ cup sugar

2 tsp baking powder

½ tsp baking soda

½ tsp salt

½ tsp nutmeg

1 cup buttermilk

1 egg, beaten

½ tsp vanilla extract

Oil of choice, for frying

Confectioners' sugar, for dusting

Directions

1. In a medium bowl, combine 2¾ cups of the flour with the sugar, baking powder, baking soda, salt, and nutmeg. Whisk everything together.

2. In a large bowl, whisk together the buttermilk, ⅓ cup water, egg, and vanilla extract. Stir in the flour mixture.

3. Use some of the remaining flour to dust your work surface. Place the dough on it and pat it into a large ½-inch-thick square. Dust the top with more flour if it gets sticky. Next, slice the dough into 2½-inch squares.

4. Now it's time to fry the beignets—be sure to ask an adult to help you! Heat 2 inches of oil in a heavy saucepan on the stovetop until the temperature reaches 325°F on a deep-fat thermometer. Check the temperature every so often while cooking. If it gets too hot, temporarily turn the heat down, or off.

5. Carefully drop 3 dough squares at a time into the hot oil. Fry them for 3 minutes, turn them over, and continue frying for 3 more minutes. Use a slotted spoon to transfer the beignets to a wire rack set atop paper towels to drain. Dust the beignets with confectioners' sugar, and enjoy!

Tip

Use a sifter or a small sieve to put the sugar on the top of the beignets.

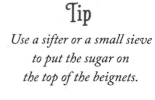

Cinnamon Swirl Coffee Cake

***** ...

Serves 10 to 12

Ingredients

Butter for greasing the baking pan

Cinnamon Filling

⅓ cup brown sugar

4 Tbsp softened butter

2 Tbsp flour

1 Tbsp cinnamon

Coffee Cake

3 cups flour

2 tsp baking powder

½ tsp baking soda

½ tsp salt

1½ cups sugar

½ cup butter, softened

3 eggs

2 tsp vanilla extract

1 (16-oz) container sour cream

Confectioners' sugar, for dusting

As a trumpet-playing gator, Louis is full of surprises—just like this coffee cake! When you take a bite, you'll find cinnamon streusel swirled through the middle.

Directions

1. Heat the oven to 350°F. Grease a 12-cup Bundt pan, making sure you get into all the grooves.

2. Combine the ingredients for the cinnamon filling in a bowl and blend them with your fingertips until the mixture resembles coarse crumbs. In another bowl, combine the flour, baking powder, baking soda, and salt. Set both mixtures aside.

3. In a large bowl, use a wooden spoon to mix the sugar into the butter until soft and smooth. Beat in the eggs one at a time. Then beat in the vanilla extract and sour cream. Add the flour mixture a little at a time, beating well after each addition.

4. Spoon half of the coffee cake batter into the Bundt pan and sprinkle the cinnamon filling on top. Pour in the remaining batter. Drag a butter knife back and forth through the batter to swirl in the cinnamon.

5. Ask an adult for help with the oven. Bake the coffee cake for 50 to 60 minutes, until a toothpick inserted in the center of the cake comes out clean. Let the cake cool in the pan for 10 minutes. Then ask an adult to help you invert it onto a wire rack to cool completely. Dust the top with confectioners' sugar.

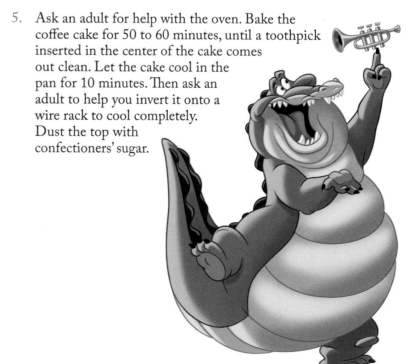

110

Simple Sugar Cookies

At her restaurant, Tiana puts her own spins on classic dishes. You can do the same with these cookies by decorating them however you like!

Directions

1. Whisk together the flour and salt in a small bowl. Set it aside.

2. In a large bowl, use a wooden spoon to press the butter into the sugar until the mixture is soft and smooth. Stir in the egg, corn syrup, and vanilla extract. Then stir in the flour mixture, one-third at a time.

3. Divide the dough into two portions. Pat each portion into a disk, wrap it in plastic, and chill until firm enough to roll (1 to 2 hours).

4. Heat the oven to 375°F. Working with one disk at a time, place the chilled dough between 2 sheets of waxed paper and roll it to about ¼-inch thickness. Use cookie cutters to cut out shapes from the dough. Reroll the dough scraps and cut out more shapes.

5. Place the shapes on an ungreased baking sheet, leaving an inch between them. If you're not planning to frost the cookies, sprinkle the tops with sugar.

6. Ask an adult for help with the oven. Bake the cookies until light brown around the edges, 8 to 10 minutes. Then leave them on the baking sheet for a few minutes before transferring them to a wire rack to cool. Decorate the cooled cookies with frosting and small candies if you like.

Makes up to 4 dozen
(depending on cookie size)

Ingredients

3½ cups flour

½ tsp salt

1 cup butter, softened

⅔ cup sugar plus more for sprinkling

1 large egg

1 Tbsp light corn syrup

1 Tbsp vanilla extract

Frosting and small candies (optional)

Tip

To make these cookies your own, try decorating them with different-colored frostings and small candies!

Makes 1 dozen

Ingredients

Blue food coloring

1 cup buttercream frosting

1 dozen baked cupcakes

12 large green gumdrops

2 dozen white chocolate chips

Black decorators' icing

Tip

Try using different colors of food coloring or candies to put your own spin on this cupcake.

Froggy-in-the-Water Cupcakes

If you visit the bayou, you might just spot a few frogs peeking out of the water! Re-create the scene with these creative cupcakes.

Directions

1. Stir drops of food coloring into the frosting until you have a shade of watery blue. Frost the cupcakes.

2. For each cupcake, create a pair of frog eyes by slicing a gumdrop in half. Press a white chocolate-chip tip down into the cut surface of each gumdrop half, centering it near the bottom edge. Squirt a dab of black decorators' icing onto each chip.

3. Set the frog eyes on the cupcakes, gently pressing them partway into the frosting to hold them in place.

Chocolate Ice Cream Pie

Tiana knows that ordering just one dessert off a menu is hard! But this pie perfectly combines a few favorites: ice cream, graham cracker crust, and lots of chocolaty goodness.

Directions

1. Seal the graham crackers in a large plastic bag and crush them with a rolling pin. Stir 1½ cups of the crumbs into the melted butter. Pour the mixture into a 9-inch pie pan.

2. When the crumbs have cooled, press them against the bottom and sides of the pan to form the piecrust. Freeze the crust for 20 minutes.

3. Scoop half the ice cream into a bowl and let it soften for about 10 minutes. Then spread it in the chilled crust. Dig 8 holes in the ice cream and fill each with a tablespoon of fudge topping. Freeze the crust for another 10 minutes.

4. Stir chocolate chips into the remaining ice cream, and then spread it over the pie. Return the pie to the freezer.

5. Beat the heavy cream at high speed for 3 to 5 minutes to thicken it. Add the cocoa mix and beat for 2 more minutes or so until the cream stiffens. Spread the whipped cream evenly over the pie and sprinkle on the remaining graham cracker crumbs. Wrap the pie in plastic and freeze it for 3 to 4 hours before serving.

Serves 8

Ingredients

20 whole chocolate graham crackers

6 Tbsp melted butter

1 qt chocolate ice cream

½ cup chocolate fudge topping

½ cup semisweet chocolate chips

1 cup heavy cream

¼ cup powdered hot cocoa mix

Tip

If you want to soften ice cream right away, try microwaving it for just a few seconds.

117

Serves 6 to 8

Ingredients

½ cup butter

3 cups sliced peaches
(about 4 large peaches)

1 cup raspberries

1 cup sugar

1 cup flour

2 tsp baking powder

Pinch of salt

1 cup milk

1 tsp vanilla extract

Whipped cream or ice
cream, for topping

Berry Peachy Cobbler

This sweet cobbler perfectly blends fruit and a biscuit topping—a combo so good you'll be begging for seconds.

Directions

1. Heat the oven to 350°F. Use a pat of the butter to grease a cast-iron skillet (or a 2½-quart casserole dish). Set the skillet aside. Ask an adult for help at the stove. Melt the remaining butter in a saucepan over low heat. Remove the pan from the stove and set it aside.

2. Combine the peaches and raspberries in a medium bowl and sprinkle 1 tablespoon of the sugar over them. Gently stir the fruit and then set it aside.

3. In a separate bowl, whisk together the flour, baking powder, and salt. Add the remaining sugar, the milk, and the vanilla extract. Stir until the mixture is evenly blended.

4. Pour the melted butter into the batter and stir quickly but gently to mix it in. Immediately pour the batter into the skillet. Add the fruit with its juices, spooning it evenly into the pan and lightly pressing it partway into the batter with a spatula.

5. Ask an adult for help with the oven. Bake the cobbler until the top is golden brown, about 1 hour. Serve warm with ice cream or whipped cream.

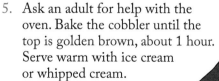

Alligator Cake

Inspired by Louis, the trumpet-playing gator, this playful cake is just as fun as a jazzy Firefly Five performance.

Directions

1. Cut the cake into 3 equal pieces. Slice one of the pieces in half at a 45-degree angle. Arrange the cake pieces on a tray or platter to create a curvy alligator body. Use one of the angled halves, placed cut-side down, for the tail. Slice the other angled half into 4 equal-size pieces for feet.

2. Stir drops of food coloring into the frosting until you have a deep shade of green. Frost the entire cake.

3. Cut the marshmallow in half and place the halves on the cake for eyeballs. Press a malted milk ball up against each eyeball for a pupil, using a dab of frosting to stick it in place. Press 2 more malted milk balls onto the alligator's snout for nostrils. Press gummy spearmint leaves and green chocolate candies into the frosting along the body for scales, and add spearmint-leaf toes to each foot.

4. Lastly, break the yogurt-covered pretzels into pieces and stick them into the frosting along the front of the cake to create alligator teeth.

Serves 10 to 12

Ingredients

10-inch baked Bundt cake

1 (16-oz) can white frosting

Green food coloring

Large marshmallow

4 malted milk balls

Gummy spearmint leaves

Green candy-coated chocolates

White-yogurt-covered pretzels

Serves 8 to 10

Ingredients

Butter for greasing
the pan

9 cups dry French bread,
in 1-inch cubes

1 cup pineapple cubes

½ cup raisins

1 tsp cinnamon

½ tsp nutmeg

Pinch of salt

3 cups milk

5 Tbsp butter

½ cup packed light
brown sugar

3 large eggs

½ tsp vanilla extract

Caramel sauce or
whipped cream

Tip

*If the bread you're
using isn't dry,
toast the cubes
lightly on a baking sheet
in the oven
before mixing them
with the other ingredients.*

Pineapple Bread Pudding

Like most bread puddings, this one is flavored with cinnamon and nutmeg. But in New Orleans, bread pudding has a special ingredient: bits of juicy pineapple.

Directions

1. Heat the oven to 350°F. Grease an 8-inch-square baking pan.

2. Combine the bread cubes, pineapple cubes, and raisins in a large mixing bowl. Sprinkle the cinnamon, nutmeg, and salt over the bread and fruit. Toss all the ingredients with a wooden spoon to mix them.

3. Ask an adult for help at the stove. Combine the milk and butter in a medium saucepan and warm them over medium-low heat until the butter melts. Remove the pan from the heat and stir in the light brown sugar.

4. Pour the milk mixture over the bread and stir until all the cubes are moistened. Let the bread stand for 5 minutes to absorb the liquid.

5. In a small bowl, whisk together the eggs and the vanilla extract. Gently stir the eggs into the bread mixture.

6. Ask an adult for help with the oven. Pour the pudding into the greased pan and bake it for 45 to 50 minutes. Serve the pudding warm, cut into squares, and topped with caramel sauce or whipped cream.

Perfect Pralines

These melt-in-your-mouth treats are just as sweet as Tiana's mama, Eudora. Making a batch is a simple process, but perfecting them can be a little tricky. New Orleans candy makers and experienced home cooks can easily prepare a batch just by using their senses to tell them when to move to the next step, but for the best results, you should use a candy thermometer and ask for help from a grown-up.

Directions

1. Line two baking sheets with parchment paper. Ask an adult for help at the stove. In a heavy-bottom pot, over medium heat, stir together both sugars, along with the evaporated milk and butter. Continue to cook, stirring occasionally, until the sugar is dissolved.

2. Bring the mixture to a boil (do not turn up the heat). Continue to cook, stirring vigorously, until the mixture reaches soft-ball stage, a temperature of 240°F. Remove from the heat and, working quickly, stir in the vanilla extract, salt, and pecans. Cook, stirring, until the mixture stiffens slightly, about 1 minute more.

3. Quickly drop a tablespoon-size portion of the mixture onto a prepared baking sheet. If it begins to set up (harden) quickly, continue to scoop and drop portions of the mixture onto the sheets. If it doesn't set up, continue to stir the mixture one or two minutes more, then try again. Let the candies cool completely before eating.

Makes 1 dozen

Ingredients

1 cup white sugar

1 cup light brown sugar

¾ cup evaporated milk

4 Tbsp (½ stick) unsalted butter

½ tsp vanilla extract

Pinch of salt

1¼ cup roasted pecans, roughly chopped

Tip

Before you start, have everything you need measured and prepared so you can work quickly.

Ingredients

2 egg whites

¼ tsp cream of tartar

⅛ tsp almond extract

½ cup sugar

Green food coloring

Sugar sprinkles

Tip

*Once the meringues
are in the oven,
keep the door closed while
they cook and cool—any
sudden change in
temperature can
cause cracks.*

Magic Meringues

Turning egg whites and sugar into fluffy meringue is nearly as magical as the moment when Tiana transforms into a princess. To do it, you'll need to whip the ingredients with an electric mixer, which will give them a light and billowy texture.

Directions

1. Heat the oven to 200°F and line a baking sheet with parchment paper.

2. With a stand or hand mixer set at medium speed, whisk the egg whites until frothy, about 1 minute. With the mixer still running, add the cream of tartar, almond extract, and a tablespoon of the sugar and blend well. Continue whisking the eggs and adding the sugar 1 tablespoon at a time and pausing between additions, until stiff peaks form, about 8 minutes more. Blend in a few drops of green food coloring.

3. Place the meringue in a piping bag fitted with a large star tip. Pipe the meringues into 1½-inch-wide dollops, spacing them 2 inches apart. Sprinkle the meringues with the sugar sprinkles. Ask an adult for help with the oven. Place the pans in the oven and bake 2 hours. Turn the oven off and let the meringues cool undisturbed, about 2 hours more. Keep in an airtight container until ready to serve.

Step-by-Step Instructions

Tiana knows that when it comes to cooking, practice makes perfect! Turn the page for step-by-step photos for a few recipes—and you'll be a pro at creating dishes that are both delicious and beautiful in no time.

Fruity Froggy Toast

Frog Shape Tutorial

Turn an apple into the perfect fruity frog shape (from page 22) with these step-by-step instructions. Make sure to ask an adult for help with the paring knife!

1. Cut two rounded sides from the apple.

2. Trim the two remaining sides of the apple.

3. With help from an adult, use a paring knife to carve a mouth into the center of each rounded side.

4. Trim away 1 inch from the end of each remaining side and halve them lengthwise, as shown.

See the full recipe on page 22!

Slithering Snake Snack

Snake Shape Tutorial

Transform a cucumber into a slithering snake (from page 92) with these step-by-step instructions. Make sure to ask an adult for help with the paring knife!

1. Trim a 1½-inch length from one end of the cucumber. Cut a wedge from the piece to form the mouth, as shown.

2. Thinly slice the remaining cucumber, reserving one slice.

See the full recipe on page 92!

Pimento Cheese Bugs

Eyes and Antenna Tutorial

Create perfect eyes and antenna for your cheese bugs (from page 94) with these step-by-step instructions.

1. Use the end of a plastic straw to cut the black olives into twelve pairs of eyes.

2. Use a toothpick to poke two holes in the side of each green olive, then slide a chive into each opening, as shown.

See the full recipe on page 94!

Magical Menus

Tiana put a lot of thought into creating the menu for her restaurant, Tiana's Palace. And she knows that combining multiple courses can often make for the most delicious meal.

Now it's your turn to put a menu together. Take a look at these magical menus that each combine a few different dishes from this cookbook—then try creating your own!

Bayou Brunch

Big Easy Mini Frittatas 18

Baked Caramel French Toast 26

Transforming Fruit Salad 82

• • •

New Orleans Favorites

Muffuletta Sandwich 32

Chicken and Sausage Gumbo 48

Tiana-Style Beignets 108

• • •

Enchanted Eats

Princess Flatbread Pizza 44

Blueberry Sparkler 104

Magic Meringues 126

• • •

A Festive Night at Tiana's Palace

Musical Meatloaf 60

Confetti Corn 78

Shrimp Dip 88

Glossary

A

Andouille sausage—a type of smoked sausage, made of pork

B

Baguette—a long, narrow loaf of French bread with a crisp crust

Bake—to cook ingredients in an oven

Baking sheet—a flat metal pan for baking cookies, biscuits, or breads

Beat—to quickly stir an ingredient or batter with a whisk, electric mixer, or spoon until it is smooth and/or fluffy

Beignet—a square-shaped pastry made of fried dough and topped with powdered sugar

Blend—to combine two or more ingredients into a smooth mixture

Bread pudding—a bread-based dessert, often made by combining leftover or stale bread with other ingredients

C

Cajun seasoning—a blend of zesty, spicy flavors, often used to cook traditional New Orleans dishes

Casserole dish—a glass or ceramic dish used for cooking and serving foods

Celery salt—a flavored salt made with ground celery seeds

Chop—to cut an ingredient into pieces that are roughly the same size

Chorizo—a type of sausage, made of pork

Confectioners' sugar—a finely ground form of sugar, also known as powdered sugar

Cornmeal—a coarse flour made of ground corn

Cream—to blend ingredients, typically butter and sugar, into a soft and creamy mixture

Cream of tartar—a dry powder often used in baking

Creole seasoning—a blend of zesty flavors that is slightly milder than Cajun seasoning, often used to cook traditional New Orleans dishes

Crumbled—broken or rubbed into small pieces

D

Dash—a small amount of an ingredient, such as lemon juice or cinnamon, added to a recipe from the container with a quick shake of the wrist

Dice—to cut foods into small cubes (typically ¼ inch wide)

Dill—a sweet herb harvested from the flowering tops of dill plants

Dressed—a New Orleans term used to order a po'boy topped with all the condiments

Drizzle—to slowly pour a thin stream of liquid or a melted ingredient over another food

Dust—to lightly sprinkle a powdery ingredient, such as confectioners' sugar or flour. Rolling pins are often dusted with flour to keep them from sticking to piecrust, cookie dough, or other foods that are rolled out.

E

Evaporated milk—a canned form of milk that includes less water than regular milk

Extract—a concentrated flavoring made by soaking certain foods, such as vanilla beans, in water and/or other liquids

F

Fillet—a piece of fish or meat from which the bones have been removed

Fold—to gently blend ingredients by using a spatula to cut through the middle of the batter and then flip the left half of the batter over onto the right half. Stiff beaten egg whites are often folded, rather than stirred, into cake and soufflé recipes to keep as much air in the batter as possible.

G

Garnish—to decorate a prepared recipe with an herb, fruit, or other edible ingredient that adds color and/or texture

Grate—to shred foods, such as coconut, carrots, cheese, or chocolate, into bits or flakes by rubbing them against a grater

Grits—a type of porridge made from ground grains, like cornmeal

Ground—when a dry ingredient has been broken up into very small pieces, often with a powderlike texture

Gumbo—a strongly flavored savory stew that is popular in Louisiana

K

Kitchen shears—scissors made specifically for cutting food

Knead—to repeatedly fold and press together dough until it is smooth and stretchy. Kneading traps air bubbles produced by the yeast, which is what makes the dough rise.

M

Meringue—a type of candy traditionally made with whipped egg whites and sugar

Mince—to chop ingredients, such as garlic cloves, gingerroot, or fresh herbs, extra fine. This evenly distributes the flavor in the dish you are cooking.

Muffuletta—a type of sandwich originated by Italian Americans in New Orleans

P

Paprika—a spice made from ground dried bell or chili peppers

Parchment paper—heat-resistant paper used to line a baking sheet so cookies and other foods won't stick to the pan when you bake them

Paring knife—a small utensil used to delicately peel or cut fruits and vegetables

Pat—to gently tap dough with the palm of your hand

Pimento cheese—a spread made with a combination of cheese, mayonnaise, and pepper

Pinch—a small amount of a dry ingredient, such as salt or a ground spice, added to a recipe with your fingertips

Po'boy—a traditional New Orleans sandwich, often made with roast beef

Praline—a type of candy traditionally made with nuts

Produce—fresh fruits and vegetables

Puree—to blend food until it is completely smooth

R

Ramekin—a small round or oval baking dish that is oven safe

Remoulade—a cold sauce, often used as a dip or condiment

Roux—a mixture made of flour and oil cooked together, used to thicken sauces or stews, like gumbo

S

Saucepan—a deep pan with a long handle and a cover that is meant for cooking foods on a stovetop

Sauté—to quickly cook food on the stovetop in a lightly oiled pan

Scallion—a long-necked onion with a small bulb

Seltzer water—water that has been combined with carbon dioxide, making it bubbly

Separate egg whites—to divide egg whites from their yolks. To do this, remove the top half of the eggshell so that both the yolk and white are still in the bottom half. Working over a bowl, slide the yolk from one half of the shell to the other, letting the egg white fall into the bowl underneath. Pour the yolk into a separate bowl.

Sifter—a utensil used for sprinkling dry ingredients onto dishes

Simmer—to cook food on the stovetop in liquid heated just to the point at which small bubbles rise to the surface

Skillet—a flat-bottomed type of frying pan with a long handle

Slaw—a kind of salad combining shredded cabbage with a dressing or condiment

Snip—to use kitchen scissors to cut an ingredient into small pieces

Soften—to warm butter (either by setting it out at room temperature or heating it in a microwave) until it is easy to combine with a mixture

Sprig—a small piece of an herb, usually including the full stem

Steep—to soak tea in water or other liquid so that flavor will be absorbed

Stock—a savory cooking liquid often used as a base for soups and sauces

Strain—to remove the liquid from food by pouring it into a colander, metal sieve, or cheesecloth. The juice or broth passes through the sieve, and the solids are retained.

Streusel—a crumbled topping or filling for baked goods, often made with cinnamon

T

To taste—just enough of a certain ingredient, usually salt, to improve the flavor of a recipe

W

Whip—to beat air into an ingredient, such as cream or egg whites, until it is light and fluffy

Whisk—a long-handled kitchen utensil with a series of wire or plastic loops at the end used to rapidly beat eggs, cream, or other liquids. *Whisk* is also a verb that means "to use a whisk."

Worcestershire sauce—a savory condiment often used to add flavor to dishes

Z

Zest—a flavorful ingredient created from the outermost rinds (or peels) of citrus fruits, like lemons, limes, and oranges. To zest a citrus fruit, ask an adult for help to find the right kitchen tool, like a zester or a box grater. Hold the fruit over a bowl and use the zester or grater to gently scrape the outer peel, turning the fruit when you reach the white part of the peel.

Index